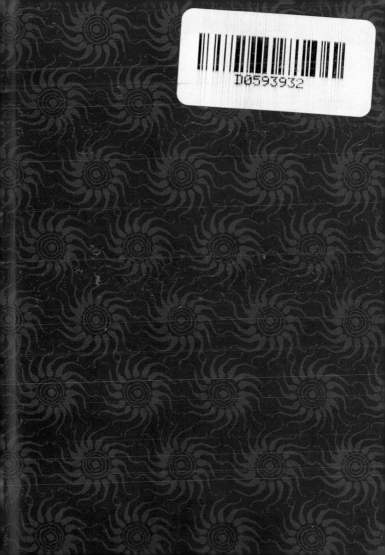

Dream Interpretation

by Lauren David Peden

THE MYSTICAL ARTS

Illustrations by Jenny Tylden Wright

WARNER ⓦ TREASURES

PUBLISHED BY WARNER BOOKS

A TIME WARNER COMPANY

Warner Treasures is a
trademark of Warner Books, Inc.

Warner Books, Inc.,
1271 Avenue of the Americas,
New York, NY 10020

W A Time Warner Company

Printed in China
First Printing: March 1996
10 9 8 7 6 5 4 3 2 1

ISBN: 0-446-91015-5

Dream Interpretation

THE MYSTICAL ARTS

Since the dawn of time, human beings have been delighted and disturbed by their dreams, and have struggled to decipher just what these nocturnal flights of fancy mean. While we sleep, we can experience an ephemeral wonder-world of surreal, fantastical illusion. Even those of us who are uninspired by day can become downright poetic at night, soaring effortlessly above the clouds, scaling the highest mountain peak, and wrestling with untamed beasts.

Dreaming is also one of the oldest forms of divination. Today, however, most dream theorists believe that our night visions are a form of psychic homework that occurs while we sleep. Dreams sort out our unfinished emotional business, and they help us assimilate new information and integrate it with preexisting knowledge. While the experts don't agree on precisely *why* we dream, one thing is certain: All living creatures dream every night, with the curious exception of the spiny anteater.

1

WHAT YOUR DREAMS
CAN TEACH YOU

If dreams are the language of the sub-conscious mind, then dreamers are the authors of their own nocturnal fantasies. In the past, dreams have inspired countless works of fiction, including Mary Shelley's *Frankenstein*, Robert Louis Stevenson's *Dr. Jekyll and Mr. Hyde*, and Bram Stoker's *Dracula*. Richard Wagner derived the opening melody of his opera *Das Rheingold* from a particularly melodious dream.

Dreams are intensely personal, like fin-gerprints, and no two are ever alike. But there are certain scenarios and symbols that most of us have experienced at least once. The most common dream situations are: falling; being chased or menaced; chasing something; being unprepared for an exam; flying; and being naked in public (Paging Dr. Freud!).

There are also certain rules of thumb to keep in mind when attempting to interpret any dream: Moving up (a staircase, a mountain, the Pyramids) indicates progress and achievement; going down signifies reverses; clean or shiny objects (or clear weather) are good omens; dirty or dull objects (or foul weather) represent obstacles or difficulties; successful efforts (whether piloting a spaceship or fighting off a swarm of killer bees) forecast success; unsuccessful efforts forecast defeat; being in a vehicle (be it a car, bus, plane, or train) symbolizes advancement, particularly if you're driving (traveling as a passenger indicates a lack of control over your own destiny); and if a dream is termed "contrary," it means the exact opposite of what you'd normally think (attending a funeral, for instance, is a dream of contrary that forecasts good news).

Finally, prophetic dreams generally fall into one of four categories: precognitive (forecasting important events); warning (suggesting the possible nature of an impending danger); factual (simply confirming or emphasizing a situation that the dreamer is already aware of); and inspirational (suggesting a solution or course of action the dreamer may not have considered).

The prophetic power of dreams has been attested to by highly noteworthy people throughout history. Consider: Joan of Arc predicted her death through a dream, as did Abraham Lincoln, who dreamed of his assassination just three days before he was shot by John Wilkes Booth. And Mark Twain had a dream of his brother's death in a boating accident at the *exact moment* it occurred!

LOGGING YOUR DREAMS

Dreams that may give us a glimpse into the future occur while we're in the deepest part of sleep (usually between 2 A.M. and 7 A.M.), and since they begin to fade from memory within fifteen minutes after we wake up, it's important to write down everything you remember as soon as you arise. Keep a pad and pencil near your bed (or a tape recorder), and grab them as soon as you open your eyes. Jot down any themes, symbols, dialogue, and emotions that come to you, but don't worry about finding the exact words to describe a complex situation or mood. Once you've got the basic information, you can always go back and elaborate on it.

A dream journal helps you refer back to previous dreams—and your interpretations of them—to chart growth and development in all areas of your life. And remember: when it comes to deciphering a dream, there are no minutiae too minute and no trivia too trivial; you have to take into consideration the surroundings, situation, and any and all noteworthy observations.

Usually one main feature will stand out in your mind, and that's what you should concentrate on first, of course, but it's the peripheral elements that help flesh out the interpretation. For instance, if you dreamed that in the middle of a lovely dinner with your spouse the two of you got into a huge screamfest, "Fight" is probably the first factor you'll pounce on—and rightly so. But you should also consider what foods or beverages were being consumed; whether or not there were flowers on the table; the color of your clothing (or the linens); and whether you were dining at home or in a crowded restaurant.

Also be aware that dreams that occur while you're sick (or after you've overindulged in alcohol, drugs, or even too-rich foods) are of no real significance. Also, persistently recurring dreams usually have their roots in a physical or psychological problem and have no prophetic value (although you might want to take them up with your shrink).

The final and most important factor to remember when practicing dream interpretation is that you are your own best guide. No one knows you as well as you know yourself, so don't be afraid to trust your instincts. If a particular symbol or reading seems to have career connotations, but you just know that it's referring to your relation-ship with Mom, you're probably right. The bottom line: Keep a careful record, consider all the details, and, ultimately, let your intuition be your guide. Sweet dreams!

METAPHORS IN MOTION: SLUMBER SYMBOLS FROM

ABANDONMENT: A dream of being abandoned means that you rarely stand up for yourself in relationships; if you left, expect to hear good news on the financial front.

ABUNDANCE: An abundance of anything symbolizes overwhelming responsibilities; steady on and you'll do fine.

ACCIDENT: A dream of an accident is usually a warning to avoid whatever was involved (a knife, car, train, plane, stairs, etc.) for the next day or so. If that's not possible, be especially careful.

AIRPLANE: An airplane represents progress and achievement. Piloting the plane yourself indicates that you're the master of your own destiny; traveling as a

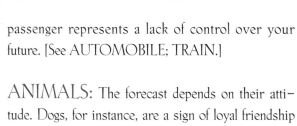

passenger represents a lack of control over your future. [See AUTOMOBILE; TRAIN.]

ANIMALS: The forecast depends on their attitude. Dogs, for instance, are a sign of loyal friendship and good luck, but a snarling, barking dog is anything but. Bears and squirrels represent career competitors; cats and foxes imply deceit and treachery; and deer suggest hesitation. If the animals were calm, you'll be successful in your affairs; if they attack you—or each other—expect the opposite (unless you were able to drive them off or overpower them). [See HORSE; LION; RABBIT; REPTILE; RODENT.]

AUTOMOBILE: As with any mode of transportation, a car suggests change and personal progress. Driving it yourself indicates that you've taken the future into your own hands; riding as a passenger implies some passivity on your part. If you had trouble controlling the car (or if it broke down), expect a few bumps on the road to success. [See AIRPLANE; TRAIN.]

AUTUMN: Dreaming of autumn in season has no real meaning, but a dream about it any other time portends benign forces around you when you need them most. A dream of getting married in autumn denotes a happy, fulfilling home life.

BABY: A dream of seeing a happy, healthy baby indicates contentment and success; a crying or sick baby means failure or disappointment. A woman who dreams of having a baby will realize a long-held ambition, and a baby taking its first steps denotes independence.

BEACH: The interpretation of a beach dream varies according to detail: Was it sunny or raining? Clear or foggy? Was the ocean calm or rough? Lying on the beach is a dream of contrary: It signifies that you'll soon be overwhelmed by a new responsibility (it can also signal an overwhelming need to "get away from it all").

BED: A dream of sleeping in your own bed promises security; a strange bed means a change (for the better) in business affairs. Making a bed portends a new lover, enjoyable occupation, or unexpected visitors.

BELLS: The interpretation depends on the dreamer's impression of the sound. If the bells struck you as ringing joyously, this heralds welcome news; if they were perceived as tolling death knells, this is not a fortuitous sign.

BICYCLE: A bicycle represents your own efforts in reaching a goal. As with any climbing dream, riding uphill signifies high hopes, and riding downhill indicates discouragement. Falling off a bicycle is a sign of failure.

BIRDS: Birds on the wing are a sign of good fortune, independence, and prosperity. Singing, gaily colored

birds imply happiness, while a dead or wounded bird warns of impending worries.

BLOOD: Be prepared for hard times if you saw blood in your dream. Bloodstained clothing represents business rivals; bloody wounds represent physical ailments and mental anxiety.

BOAT: A boat symbolizes your life and ambitions; to interpret the dream you need to consider the weather, the condition of the water, and any other pertinent details. Basically, though, if the boat was moving easily through calm water, the outlook is good; if the water was rough or choppy, or the boat was damaged, the outlook is dicey. [See SAILING.]

BOOKS: Studying or reading books signifies forthcoming honors and a calm, pleasant future. [See READING.]

BOX: An empty box augurs frustration and upset plans, while a full box signifies wealth and the ability to surmount obstacles.

BRIDE: This is a good luck omen if you saw or were the bride (in the latter case, there's an inheritance in your immediate future). Kissing a bride portends a reconciliation between friends. [See MARRY; WEDDING.]

BRIDGE: Crossing over a bridge symbolizes triumph

over problems. Going under a bridge implies that additional problems are headed your way.

BURIAL: This is a dream of contrary. If you attended a burial, expect news of a wedding or birth. A dream of being buried alive, however, is a warning against unethical behavior and the temptation to underestimate a business opponent. [See CEMETERY; FUNERAL.]

CANDLES: Lit candles are an optimistic omen and signify a bright future; unlit candles foretell sad news about a friend or loved one.

CAVE: Being trapped in a cave is an obstacle dream foreshadowing change or warning of a problem that will warrant your attention. If you found your way out, you'll quickly overcome present difficulties, but if you were unable to escape, expect your troubles to escalate. [See TUNNEL.]

CELLAR: A dry, well-stocked cellar heralds success and contentment in love and business; a dank, empty cellar augurs bad news and disappointments. Being trapped in a cellar, as in the case of a cave, portends serious anxiety, and possibly even illness.

CEMETERY: A clean, well-kept cemetery is a dream of contrary heralding unexpected good news (from a long-lost friend, perhaps). If the cemetery was run down or overgrown, a bit of bad luck may precede the good. A coffin is almost always a negative symbol, and seeing yourself inside one implies repression or defeat. [See BURIAL; FUNERAL.]

CHASE: One of the most common dreams involves being pursued, either by a person (or crowd), animal(s), or natural disaster such as an avalanche or flood. This dream is your subconscious's way of alerting you to a hidden problem or phobia that needs to be addressed and dealt with. [See CAVE; ESCAPE; JAIL.]

CHILDREN: A dream featuring children portends domestic bliss and great prosperity—whichever concerns you most.

CLIMB: The act of climbing or moving upward—on a mountain, hill, ladder, stairs, elevator, or escalator—indicates that you're overcoming obstacles on the path to success (even if the effort of doing so was taxing). If you're moving (or falling) downward, however, setbacks are likely to occur.

CLOUDS: Dark storm clouds symbolize confusion, and are predictive of misfortune and sorrow due to a broken friendship or unfortunate business deal. If you saw the sun through passing white clouds, your troubles will soon pass, as well. White clouds themselves are thought to forecast travel.

COLORS: A mix of colors (as in a rainbow) is a sign of great good luck and happiness. If you only saw one color (or one stood out), it means the following: **Bright red** warns against unnecessary anger; **deep red** forecasts unexpected good news and an active future; **blue** is indicative of a peaceful home life free from worry; **green** pertains to travel and moneymaking capabilities; **brown** augurs money luck (and a possible accusation of dishonesty); **orange** stands for home ownership and stalled plans; **purple** promises great sociability and a comfortable lifestyle; **yellow** denotes jealousy and obstacles; **black** is a general omen of bad luck or difficulties to be overcome; and **white** portends success and distinction. The brighter the color, the more accurate the forecast.

CONCERT: A highbrow concert forecasts a profitable business season. A dream of attending a play or concert can also suggest a yen for a creative outlet of expression, while a dream of actually performing indicates that your creative potential is being fulfilled.

CROWD: An orderly, well-dressed crowd denotes fortuitous friendships and opportunities for growth, but if they were unhappy in any way, expect the opposite. If you had to yell to be heard in a crowd, this indicates that you'll put your own interests before those of others.

D

DANCING: Dancing yourself heralds unexpected good fortune; if other people were dancing, expect a change for the better in affairs of the heart. Dancing children denote a cheerful home life, and seeing older people cut a rug signifies the end of money woes.

DANGER: If you faced down a threatening opponent, you'll overcome any problems that are impeding your success. If you didn't, expect your current troubles to continue.

DARKNESS: If you were surrounded by darkness, prepare for delays and setbacks (unless you found your way into the light, or there were bright stars or moonlight in the night sky, which indicates eventual success). [See MOON; NIGHT.]

DAWN: A clear break of day forecasts new opportunities that will lead to success; however, if the dawn was rainy or grey, unexpected disappointment will follow. [See LIGHT; MORNING.]

DEATH: If you dream of death only occasionally, it's just a reaction to an unpleasant event, but if you repeatedly dream of your own death, a medical checkup is in order. Studies have shown that such dreams often signal a cardiac condition of which the dreamer may be unaware.

DEVIL: Devils and demons represent enemies, so if you fought him (or them) off and escaped from harm, you'll defeat your adversaries. If you didn't, expect the opposite. If the devil speaks to you, you'll have to work hard to resist some temptation.

DOOR: This is an obstacle dream. If the door was open and you were able to pass through, this signifies that you'll easily reach a favored goal; if it was stuck, locked, or otherwise unpassable, your efforts are for naught. [See GATE.]

DRINKING: The interpretation depends on the beverage in question. **Beer** forecasts a new undertaking; **wine** portends happiness and prosperity; **carbonated drinks** predict exciting events in the near future; **milk** signifies good health and success (unless it's sour, which denotes disappointment); **water**, if clear and cold, is a favorable omen of achievement (while warm, murky water forecasts the opposite); a good cup of **coffee** heralds unexpected good news (bitter java means problems in a friendship); and **orange juice** foretells a brief—but passionate—love affair.

DROWN: A dream of drowning is an unfortunate omen pertaining to financial and business situations. If you were rescued, you'll recoup your losses with the help of a friend.

DUSK: The fading sun of early evening suggests an ending of some kind (and unrealized hopes, along with it). [See EVENING.]

E

EATING: In general, eating in pleasant company is a fortunate omen, while eating alone signals future loneliness. The interpretation also depends on what you were eating. Eating an **apple** can symbolize romance (or trouble in Paradise, à la Adam and Eve); foods eaten in groups (**peas, corn, beans, stew, cereals**) represent group activities and the accumulation of wealth; fruits that must be peeled (**oranges, lemons, grapefruit,** and **bananas**) epitomize secrets and difficulties in love and career matters; **rice** denotes domestic comfort and communal bonding; **berries** and **grapes** have erotic connotations and also predict a comfortable lifestyle; **meat** is a good omen (unless it's spoiled); **sugar** foretells the end of a troubling issue; **eggs** denote good health, **raisins** symbolize questionable business associates and a possible cash flow problem; eating **soup** forecasts financial ease; and eating **fish** portends loyal friendships.

EGGS: Eggs are an omen of general good fortune. Eggs in a bird's nest predict an inheritance or financial windfall, and fresh eggs denote happy circumstances ahead. Cracked or rotten eggs warn of future disappointments through misplaced trust.

EMBARRASSMENT: In this dream of contrary, the greater your embarrassment, the more profoundly satisfying your imminent success will be.

ESCAPE: Escaping from a place of confinement predicts straightforward success through hard work; escaping from a natural disaster (fire or water) suggests that your success will follow a period of anxiety; escaping from an animal suggests there's an underhanded "friend" in your midst. If you tried to escape and failed, expect setbacks due to duplicitous associates; and if you failed outright, be prepared to slog through a trying episode. [See CAVE; CHASE; JAIL.]

EVENING: A pleasant evening portends a sense of fulfillment in middle and old age. A dream of seeing stars in the evening sky is a sign of exploration and great potential. [See DUSK.]

FACE: A bright, smiling face signifies happiness and friendship. A sad or ugly face denotes troubles and arguments; seeing your own face portends unhappiness; and washing your face suggests repentance for past misdeeds.

FALLING: Falling is the most common action in dreams, and is symbolic of a basic (largely subconscious) fear—sexual, moral, or of general inadequacies—that the dreamer has yet to come to terms with. Prophetically speaking, the meaning of this dream depends on its outcome: If you fell from a great height and were not hurt, expect temporary setbacks; if you hurt yourself, you may encounter real hardships for an extended period of time. Falling from a medium height symbolizes decreased authority; tripping or falling from your seat warns against two-faced friends. If you got up after you fell, this implies that you'll be triumphant in the end.

FIGHT: Fighting in a dream signifies anger, frustration, and the desire for change. If you won, you'll overcome all obstacles to reach your goal.

FIRE: Fire is generally a favorable omen of emotional involvement, providing you weren't burned. A raging fire may symbolize a situation that has spun out of control; but a cozy fire (in a fireplace or campsite) represents stability and contentment. Seeing your house burn to the ground is a dream of contrary, forecasting a happy home life.

FISH: Fish are a sign of extreme good luck, unless they were dead, which is a portent of discouragement and ill fortune. Catching fish symbolizes your success.

FLOWERS: Brightly colored blossoms symbolize fertility and creation, and promise happiness, prosperity, and contentment. Withered or dead flowers are a sign of adversity and illness.

FLYING: Flying is representative of the dreamer's ambition. If you soared effortlessly, you'll achieve your goal with ease. If flying was difficult, this implies that there are still hurdles to overcome and that your reach may exceed your grasp. A dream of flying may also symbolize the dreamer's delight over a recent accomplishment.

FOG: Being surrounded by fog or mist indicates confusion or uncertainty; dense fog on land symbolizes business or financial worries, while fog at

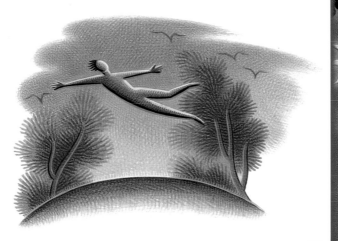

sea is indicative of romantic or domestic dilemmas. If the fog lifted during your dream, success is inevitable.

FOREST: Stately trees with lush foliage promise relief from stress and financial gains; being lost in a forest symbolizes confusion. [See TREES.]

FRIENDS: A dream of old friends foretells unexpected news or the recovery of something you thought you lost. Having a pleasant conversation with an acquaintance signifies tranquility at home and work; any display of loyal friendship in a dream portends happiness in social situations.

FRUIT: Ripe fruit (on the vine or table) suggests a fulfilling, financially secure future; rotten or bitter fruit is an unlucky omen. [See EATING.]

FUNERAL: A dream of seeing or attending a funeral is a dream of contrary that forecasts good news and possible monetary gains. [See BURIAL; CEMETERY.]

GARDEN: A dream of being in a garden—alone or with your lover—signals a satisfying, comfortable life and fulfilling occupation.

GATE: If the gate was closed or locked, it represents insurmountable obstacles; however, if you were able to open or get around the gate somehow, you'll find a way to surmount your problems. An open gate, of course, is indicative of great opportunity ahead. [See DOOR.]

GRASS: Green, well-tended grass signals good luck in any undertaking; dry, weedy, or withered grass predicts the reverse.

H

HAIR: Hair that was abundant and that looked and felt good is a sign of good health and contentment; being unable to detangle knotted hair is a warning against being too temperamental and critical in love relationships; thinning hair forecasts anxiety and financial difficulties; a dream that your hair turned white overnight while your face didn't age signifies disaster and overwhelming grief; trimming your hair forecasts a successful new venture.

HANDS: Clean, well-groomed hands are prophetic of great distinction and financial satisfaction; dirty, ugly hands portend defeat. Shaking hands is a sign of reconciliation; if you shook hands with someone less important than yourself, this implies that you'll be admired for your kindness.

HORSE: Dreaming of horses is a fortunate omen. Seeing a horse predicts a comfortable existence. Riding a horse uphill indicates optimism and success (the faster he gallops, the swifter your victory); but riding downhill augurs a period of disenchantment; and falling or being thrown from a horse signals defeat. Also take into consideration the color of the horse: a dark horse predicts delays and discontent; a white horse highlights the positive aspects of the dream. [See CLIMBING; COLORS.]

HOUSE: An old house, in good repair, signals a reunion or renewed association; if it's dilapidated, prepare for setbacks and failure in some area of your life. A dream of building a house is a sign that you'll make intelligent choices that will benefit you financially.

HUSBAND: If a woman dreams that her husband leaves her, they'll quarrel, then reconcile unexpectedly.

I

ICE: Walking on ice is a warning that you risk security for momentary pleasures; seeing ice floating on water is a sign that someone's jealousy will interfere with your peace of mind; slipping or falling on ice forecasts troubles of a minor nature.

INFIDELITY: A dream of being unfaithful forecasts family problems, regardless of whether or not you acted on your impulse (although the outcome is not as serious if you resisted temptation).

INJURY: Suffering a physical injury suggests that there are malevolent forces working against you: Proceed with caution.

INSANITY: A dream of being insane your-self portends trouble of a financial or business nature. If others appeared mad, prepare for an unpleasant surprise.

INSECTS: In most cases, this is an obstacle dream warning that you're surrounded by unfa-vorable influences. If you didn't get stung or were able to drive the bugs away, you'll over-come your difficulties and ultimately succeed in your endeavors. Threatening insects (**wasps, mosquitoes, scorpions**) represent dangerous situations, and **bees** and **ants** symbolize success through teamwork. **Butterflies**, however, are a favorable omen representing joy and freedom. [See SPIDER.]

J

JAIL: Being trapped in a prison cell is a common obstacle dream representative of an approaching quandary (such as running behind on a deadline or being unable to meet financial obligations) that warrants your attention. If you managed to escape, your problems will be short-lived; otherwise, expect a long and formidable struggle. [See CAVE; CHASE; ESCAPE.]

JEALOUSY: For a husband to dream that he's jealous over his wife signifies deceit on the part of a narrow-minded business or social acquaintance; envy over his lover signals that he'll wrangle with a rival. For a woman to have a jealous dream about her husband portends a thoughtless incident and subsequent squabbling; jealousy of her lover signals that she has good reason to doubt his devotion. If you feel jealous of someone other than your spouse or lover, this portends that you'll be the object of undeserved animosity that will have a negative effect on your overall relationships.

JUMPING: Jumping over any object indicates that you'll surmount hurdles and reach your goal. If you were unsuccessful in jumping over something, prepare for maddening setbacks. [See CLIMB; DOOR; GATE.]

K

KEYS: Lost keys symbolize anger and dissension; found keys indicate domestic tranquility and the resolution of a serious problem. Using a key to unlock a door can portend new opportunities in love and on the job; using a key to lock a door means you've chosen a good mate.

KISS: If the kissing was heartfelt (and not of an illicit nature), it's a token of joy and contentment; if it was meaningless or insincere, look out for a deceitful friend or unfulfilling relationship. Kissing someone passionately on the neck symbolizes immoral inclinations.

KNIVES: Not a good sign. Knives portend disagreements and separations between friends and loved ones. A rusty knife forecasts heartbreak within the family; a sharp, polished knife signifies anxiety; a dull or broken knife foretells hard work that culminates in defeat.

L

LADDER: A sign of advancement if you were ascending, while descending denotes damage (and falling foretells frustration and defeat).

LAKE: A clear, calm lake signals smooth sailing on the sea of life, but a muddy or stormy lake denotes the opposite. [See RIVER; WATER.]

LAMP: A lit lamp signifies success in romance and career; an unlit lamp denotes dissatisfaction. Carrying a lamp portends prestige and independence; and a dim or flickering lamp forecasts news of ill health. [See LIGHT.]

LETTER: If the letter you received contained good news, your future looks bright; if the news was bad, prepare for impending difficulties.

LIGHT: If daylight is featured in your dream, it promises renewed hope and improvement in your current situation. A beam of light foreshadows a sudden solution to a long-standing problem, and a dim light implies partial success. [See DAWN; LAMP; SUN.]

LION: A lion symbolizes leadership and drive. Seeing or being a lion denotes prestige and personal success. Fighting with a lion means that you'll tangle with a formidable opponent; if you subdued him, your prospects look bright; if not, expect an attack by your enemies. Young lion cubs denote new ventures and worthwhile friendships.

LOVE: A feeling of love for others means you're satisfied with your current situation (feeling loved by another person also implies a happy state of affairs). If your love was not reciprocated, prepare for a disappointment of some kind.

MARRY: For single people, a dream of being married portends that their current relationship may not be worth the effort they've invested. If a woman dreamed of marrying a much older man, she'll soon experience trouble. [See BRIDE; WEDDING.]

MIRROR: Spying your own reflection implies a desire for self-examination; seeing others in a mirror is an indication that your friends or associates may not be on the up and up. Breaking a mirror forecasts trouble; if you saw your reflection in a broken mirror, it implies that your self-image may be somewhat shattered.

MONEY: Finding money is a mixed blessing indicat-

ing that monetary success will be marred by disenchantment; losing money is a dream of contrary that portends a
possible windfall.

MOON: A new moon augurs financial coups and fun-
loving friends; a full moon forecasts a fulfilling love life; and
a moon obscured by clouds or an eclipse means that you'll
have to contend with a few obstacles before success comes
a-knockin'. A bright moon surrounded by stars indicates
adventure and exploration. [See DARKNESS; NIGHT.]

MORNING: If the morning dawns clear, it indicates
that success is close at hand; if it's cloudy, the opposite is
true. [See DAWN.]

MOUNTAIN: As with all climbing dreams, moving
up is a positive sign of solid achievement; moving down
means you'll probably take a dive. [See CLIMB.]

MUSIC: Melodious or harmonious music is an omen
of joy and good fortune; discordant or out-of-tune music
foretells, well . . . discord. [See PIANO.]

NAKEDNESS: Dreaming of being naked in public is inspired by a common fear of exposure ("I'm no good at —— [my job, relationships, whatever]. I'm a fraud. I'm going to be found out!"). It

may also be triggered by anxiety about specific nerve-wracking situations (meeting the in-laws, giving a speech). [See TEST.]

NIGHT: If you dream of night, expect obstacles and oppression; if you see bright moonlight or daybreak on the horizon, any troubles foretold in this dream will be minimized. [See DARKNESS; MOON.]

NOSE: Seeing your own nose indicates strength of character and the conviction to see things through; if your nose appears too small (or it's gone altogether), prepare for a delay in plans. A nosebleed signifies hard times and possible monetary setbacks.

OCEAN: If the ocean was calm, expect overall good luck. A choppy ocean denotes mixed fortunes, and rough waters portend rough times ahead. Swimming in the ocean signifies that you'll enjoy new responsibilities and/or activities; and swimming toward shore indicates security through hard work. [See SWIMMING; WATER.]

ODOR: Pleasant odors are a good omen; unpleasant smells foretell aggravation.

OPERATION: Going under the surgeon's knife means that a problem will only be solved by drastic measures. [See KNIFE.]

P

PARADISE: A dream of paradise augurs personal happiness and loyal friends.

PARALYSIS: If you dream that you or your lover are paralyzed, you've lost that loving feeling (and may be suffering from an emotional or sexual conflict). This dream also symbolizes a subconscious desire to buck overwhelming responsibilities.

PARENTS: A dream of both parents forecasts unusual happiness (especially if they're in good spirits). Fathers, seen alone, symbolize authority, and mothers symbolize love.

PENCIL: A dream of pencils augurs good health and a fulfilling and rewarding career.

PIANO: Tickling the ivories yourself (particularly if you don't play in reality) is a sign that you'll succeed in all your endeavors—if the instrument was out-of-tune, expect a few setbacks along the way. Hearing harmonious piano playing is also a symbol of success. [See MUSIC.]

POCKETBOOK: If you found a purse (your own or someone else's) filled with money, your financial outlook looks swell. If the purse was empty, you'll come face-to-face with discouragement in the not too distant future.

PORCH: Sitting on a porch foretells contentment and the desire to try new things.

PYRAMID: Seeing a pyramid augurs change and travel; scaling one is symbolic of achievement. [See CLIMB.]

QUARREL: A dream of contrary portending luck in love and business.

QUESTION: Making inquiries is an omen of general good fortune; if you were questioned, it can either foretell good tidings (if you were able to answer) or bad (if you choked).

QUICKSAND: If you were being sucked under, you'll be overwhelmed by adversity; if you managed to get free, your troubles will be diminished.

R

RABBIT: Rabbits are a sign of increased responsibility and the willingness to work hard (they also symbolize the increased rewards that are a by-product of your efforts).

RACE: A dream of watching or being in a race is an obstacle dream. If you (or the car, horse, person you rooted for) were victorious, you'll overcome the odds against you and succeed at a highly valued endeavor. [See CHASE; RUNNING.]

RAIN: Being caught in a clear, spring rain shower promises prosperity and all around contentment; being drenched in a sudden downpour foretells unforseen wealth; and watching rainfall from indoors augurs domestic bliss. [See STORM.]

READING: Reading in your dreams is a generally favorable omen signaling advancement and the likelihood that you'll excel at an arduous task. [See BOOKS.]

REPTILE: Alligators, snakes, and other reptiles are classic symbols of enemies. A reptile dream is a warning to be on your guard against treachery (unless you overpowered or killed it, which means you'll prevail).

RIVER: A fast-moving river represents fruitless efforts. Falling in forecasts additional difficulties, while a frozen river portends major setbacks. [See LAKE; WATER.]

ROCKING CHAIR: Occupied rocking chairs are a harbinger of contentment; empty rockers forecast a temporary period of loneliness.

RODENT: Mice, rats, and weasels symbolize insincerity and deception (unless they're white, which suggests protection through benign forces). If you killed them, you'll handily defeat your adversaries.

RUNNING: Running signifies that you're enmeshed in a situation or obligation from which you'd like to break free. Being unable to run implies a lack of confidence in your ability to overcome this current oppression. [See CHASE; RACE.]

S

SAILING: Sailing on calm waters with a steady wind promises joy and prosperity; choppy seas or dead calm predict disillusionment. [See BOAT.]

SCHOOL: A dream of attending school is indicative of overall progress and distinction in your career.

SCISSORS: Scissors are an unlucky portent of quarrels and severed relationships.

SEX: Erotic dreams are quite common, and often don't require much in the way of interpretation. Keep in mind, though, that sometimes a sex dream is more about the need for affection or a close, fulfilling relationship than it is about the deed itself.

SNOW: Finding yourself in a snowstorm is a sign that your hard work will be rewarded.

Melting snow signifies melting anxieties; watching a snowstorm portends minor problems; and watching the snow fall from inside a cozy dwelling indicates domestic bliss.

SPIDER: This arachnid symbolizes industriousness and happy domesticity (especially if it's spinning a web). Surprisingly, tarantulas are an omen of good fortune. [See INSECTS.]

SPORTS: Team sports indicate a desire to forge productive alliances; solitary pursuits signify self-reliance.

STAIRS: Walking downstairs is symbolic of frustration and setbacks; walking upstairs signifies solid achievement and progress; and falling down them forecasts failure. [See CLIMB.]

STORM: This is an obstacle dream portending discontent; if the storm passes, so will your troubles. [See RAIN.]

SUN: The sun is symbolic of life and optimism. Bright sunlight is indicative of satisfaction and overall well-being; a sunrise augurs new opportunities; sunset indicates the passage of time. [See DAWN; DUSK; LIGHT.]

SWIMMING: Swimming is a sign of good health, but if the water was dirty, expect some difficulties. If you were having fun and swimming without effort, expect an easy time ahead; swimming with difficulty portends dissatisfaction; and swimming underwater indicates anxiety. [See OCEAN; WATER.]

T

TABLE: A kitchen table symbolizes hard work; a dining table (particulary one that's set with fine china and linen) augurs close friendships and happy domesticity; a card table forecasts a chance to improve your monetary situation; and an empty table signifies loss and disagreements.

TEETH: Loose teeth forecast failure and untrustworthy friends; decayed teeth augur health problems; clean, white teeth predict fulfillment and wealth; having them pulled forecasts a favorable investment opportunity; brushing your teeth means you'll overcome ostacles; and losing or spitting out your teeth indicates that you'll face overwhelming burdens and financial setbacks. A dream that you're toothless signifies your difficulty in reaching goals.

TEST: This classic obstacle dream—being unprepared for an exam—indicates an unspoken fear that your ambitions are beyond your abilities and that you'll be "found out." The forecast of the dream depends on whether or not you passed. [See NAKED.]

TOYS: Playing with toys is a general sign of good luck denoting pleasant developments in all aspects of your life. Broken toys, however, are a warning against childish or impulsive behavior.

TRAIN: Moving forward in any vehicle (train, car, spaceship) is a sign of personal progress and goal-oriented behavior, particularly if you were driving. Losing control of the train means you fear losing control of your life, and riding as a passenger indicates a certain... passive attitude about your future destinations. [See AIRPLANE; AUTOMOBILE.]

TREES: Trees with green foliage are a sign of health and well-being; the leaves' turning color indicates change; their falling signifies loss or despair. Cutting down trees warns of wasting your energy in futile pursuits; climbing a tree symbolizes progress and achievement; and planting a tree is an omen of strong, fruitful relationships. [See FOREST.]

TUNNEL: Going through a tunnel is an obstacle dream, symbolizing the dreamer's struggle to succeed at a specific task; if you made it through, your efforts have paid off, if not, prepare for defeat. Tunnel dreams can also represent a change, risk, or opportunity that is causing you anxiety. [See CAVE.]

U

UMBRELLA: Carrying an open (and functioning) umbrella in the rain is a favorable omen of pleasure and prosperity. A leaky umbrella denotes a strained love relationship; a broken or torn umbrella bespeaks minor difficulties and forces working to delay your achievements.

UNDRESSING: A dream of undressing yourself indicates that you've misplaced your trust and affections; if others are undressing, you'll soon unravel a mystery.

V

VASE: A flower-filled vase suggests contentment; a broken vase denotes sorrow; and drinking
from a vase augurs an illicit affair.

VEGETABLES: Growing vegetables forecasts a happy home life; rotten veggies portend sadness and disappointments; and eating vegetables means you should prepare for a season of ups and downs. [See EATING.]

VOYAGE: Disaster while sailing denotes bad luck in love, but if the voyage was pleasant, an inheritance is in the offing.

WALKING: Walking with ease augurs easy triumph; walking with difficulty portends temporary obstacles on the road to success.

WATER: Clear, calm water is a favorable omen, while rough or murky water signifies troubles. Frolicking in water forecasts a sudden romantic awakening; while having water splashed or sprayed on your head portends an unusually passionate (and possibly violent) love affair. [See OCEAN; SWIMMING.]

WEDDING: Attending a wedding is symbolic of impending joy—if the wedding was a happy, uplifting affair. If it was unpleasant or somber, sadness is on the horizon. [See BRIDE; MARRY.]

WIND: Walking head-on into a strong, gusty wind indicates that you're determined to succeed in your endeavors. A stormy gale forecasts a period of hard work, and a soft, mild breeze indicates that you put love ahead of money.

WINDOW: An open window is a sign that success will come easily; a closed window indicates obstacles (unless you closed it yourself, which means you've escaped a dangerous situation), and climbing out a window suggests that you'll successfully navigate stumbling blocks. Broken windows indicate disloyal friends or loved ones.

WRITING: Writing yourself is a warning against making mistakes or acting impulsively; reading strange handwriting is a warning against financial speculation; and seeing others writing suggests that you place too much stock in other people's opinions.

X Y Z

YARN: Knitting or winding yarn into a ball forecasts a commingling of love and money.

YOUNG: Seeing young people forecasts a reconciliation with a relative; a dream that you're young again suggests that you'll go to great lengths to revitalize a missed opportunity.

ZEBRA: Zebras symbolize a fleeting but profitable enterprise.

ZIPPER: If the zipper was broken, social embarrassment is imminent; if it closed easily, a vexing matter will be resolved in your favor.

ZOO: Visiting a zoo forecasts exciting travel opportunities, and if you were accompanied by a child, your sojourn will be profitable as well as pleasurable.

PROBLEM SOLVING IN YOUR SLEEP

Whatever the scope of your problem, it is entirely possible to devise a solution while you slumber, using a technique known as *dream incubation*. It's easy: Before going to bed, write a short paragraph concerning your question or dilemma. Read the paragraph over after you've gotten into bed and condense its meaning into a single, salient sentence. Repeat this sentence like a mantra until you fall asleep. Studies have shown that this simple exercise helps direct your subconscious attention to the problem within your dreams, which you can later use to analyze the situation. When you wake up, immediately write down whatever you remember—be it a whole, cohesive dream or disjointed fragments—and see what parts apply to your particular predicament. It's like any other puzzle: If it's a match, the parts will click into place easily, and you'll be that much closer to resolving your quandary.

If your problem is of a more nerve-wracking, performance-anxiety variety—giving a big speech, say, or meeting your prospective in-laws—you might want to try something called *lucid dreaming*. Lucid dreaming was first researched by Dutch psychiatrist Frederick van Eeden in 1913, and it refers to those times when you realize that you're dreaming while you're doing it. Dream theorists now believe that lucid dreaming can be willfully developed, and that we can use it to direct the outcome of our dreams, which, in turn, may help us take greater control over our waking lives.

With a little practice, lucid dreaming can also be used to rehearse those never-let-'em-see-you-sweat moments. After you wake up in the morning, occupy yourself with some trivial activity—like reading or watching TV. Then lie down and go back to sleep; concentrate on lucidly reentering the dream that preceded your awakening. Once you've mastered this technique, you can use it to actively play out any imaginable scenario.

Now you're ready to delve into your dreams with new purpose. With practice, your nighttime visions can help you take charge of the present, and uncover the mysteries of the future. Sleep tight!